TANGERINE DREAMS

A JOURNAL OF VERSE
BY

BERLIN BURKE

Published by

CONTENTS

CHAPTER I

THE
EMPRESS

WRITTEN ON YOUR BODY

Right now,
here,
where I sit,
I have the only and best body I will ever have.
But my soul is a story told in astronomic explosions and interstellar ink.
This is the part of me I want you to see;
to hoard my knowledge,
and build a god library
on the lines of your forehead.

ECHOES

You stand before me an echo.
A mirage of long-lost mist wrapped in the knowledge of your
formation.
I count your scars without hindrance;
follow the lines etched on your face with my mouth,
and read the sorrow of your being with my tongue.
You are merely oblivion, a hope of a dream yet to be born and yet
to me you exist - the pale skin that holds you also confines you;
separates you from the sameness of me.
You are the echo
...a voice returned that speaks only to me.

~ X ~

CONFESSION OF SILENCE

Every time my heart breaks,
shatters into minuscule splinters around me;
you have been there.
You have cut your feet and bled your soul to walk the sharp edge of my life,
simply to comfort me,
to take my hand into your own,
and open my heart to the light of the sun.

You have made me laugh and made me cry from the depth of my
being.
You have wrapped yourself around me in ecstasy with only your
passion to guide you.
You were the first and will be the last to touch the tender recesses
of my naked spirit.
The one who lifted my life from the ashes, made it rise and face the
storm with the fortitude of the Phoenix.

You bring me closer to the spirit of God.
You hold me up on your own sacred pedestal and trim the edges
with your all-forgiving touch.

If I hold a hand of sand I do not see the greyness of age nor
the ravages of nature.
I simply see the flickering light of life in each particle.
I see the colours dance against the waves as I see your
intimate flame warming my mind.

You complete the physics of my mind, the chemistry of
my body.

You fill the horrifying emptiness within and create
stillness, a quiet which resonates through me and
closes me to all but you.

~ xii ~

YOUR WORDS

To find in serenity inexplicable trust, obscured by untruth, is to gaze at you in
awe of my own acknowledgment.

How far have I travelled around the labyrinth of your façade?
How did I fail to acknowledge the veneer of your patina – the marks of
your fiction?

Your apathetic terror rolls from your skin as sap from a felled giant and
sticks with ferocity to the image in your mirror.

Your vain attempt at double-edged manipulation leaves me cold,
cold as the sleet mountain ridges in my mind.
Like a snow leopard, I retreat into a sanctum of clarity – seek your
face in the crystal dawn and marvel at your ugliness.

Your doppelganger is schizophrenic; plagued by its need to feed on
the lies of your words.

You twist and turn within words – words used to pull us close and
feed on emotion – you pace your syllables as a divine source of
your own edification.

You want the world to see the difference of your
indifference and yet you fail, when observed closely, to
cover your narrative with a dose of plausibility.

The amateur would fail to notice that your prose is a
figure in the mist, gleaming like the palpable yet
missing spark which makes humans of the rest of us.

Your failure is of the reserved kind – meant only for
those who will not open their eyes to see.

SARCOPHAGUS

You built an ossuary for my sin from the sepulchre of your bones.
Inlaid it with the dead spaces between the stars.
You entombed me with lace fragments and forgotten words and left me
to dream,
to yearn.
In the solitude of my sarcophagus, I found the cliché written between our
agonies.
We understand each other's pain because we understand our own.
You are the ancient potter that filled my fissures with gold because
you find them beautiful, not fatal.
You remain the witness and I the watcher.
And still, you bring me to my knees.

NEAR EXPERIENCE

A second-hand life, like a distant heart, creates a wilderness around it.
A near-life experience haunts more than a near-death.
You are my incomplete surrender.

A void, a missing, an invalid entry... ellipses on a white page.
And yet I love you like one loves all dark things; secretly, within and from afar.
Alas, some loves are not meant to be because
the problem with liars is that they believe no one.
Yet I find solace in the thought that big dreams do not find homes in small minds.

PITTORE

Only I can decipher the longitude of your hands.
The latitude of your lips.
Hands and lips that have travelled the narrow valleys of my flesh and
abundant chasms of my mind.
Hands and lips that have sculpted my small sighs into volcanic screams.
You painted your fresco onto the canvas of my unblemished bones and
selfishly I hid its beauty with my skin.
Yet you remain my poetry,
in a world still learning
to scratch pictures onto rock face.

TANGERINE DREAM

Your rounded curves stretch before me like molten sand cast into
leaded glass.
I lift my hand in wonder and shape your eons with my eternity.
Between the lush down of your flesh and the pliable envy of your
bitter bones, I trace my nails...
until a faint tangerine line slides up the forgotten road of your ribs.

I incise my name onto your carcass and at that moment...
my soul sighs.

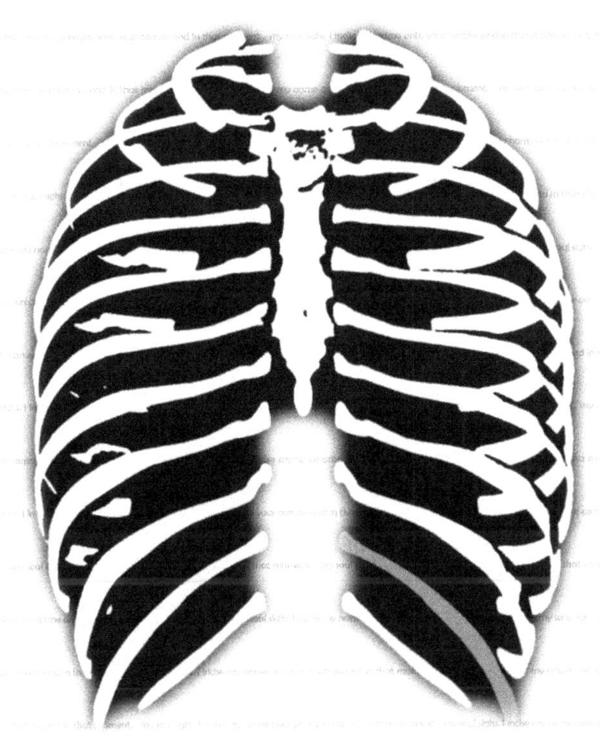

FAMILIAR

Your name
a prayer
whispered on the penitent altar of my lips.
I worship each rounded syllable of its sound.
There I find the demi-gods of my fate
etched into the holiness of your eyes.

EXPOSURE

Blood, like developing fluid, envelopes the contours of your hands and exposes them slowly;
a grainy picture emerging from the damp darkness of their hiding place.
The whiteness of your bones shines as salt through the liquid syrup of your skin
waiting for the embrace of my solitude.

ABACUS

My fingers trace your vertebrae
.... tumbling against your bones as though your damp skin were
little more than a breathing abacus.
Like an alchemist, I find the symbols of your flesh.
Count your secrets,
add your desires,
all the while searching
for the multiplicity
of your missing parts.

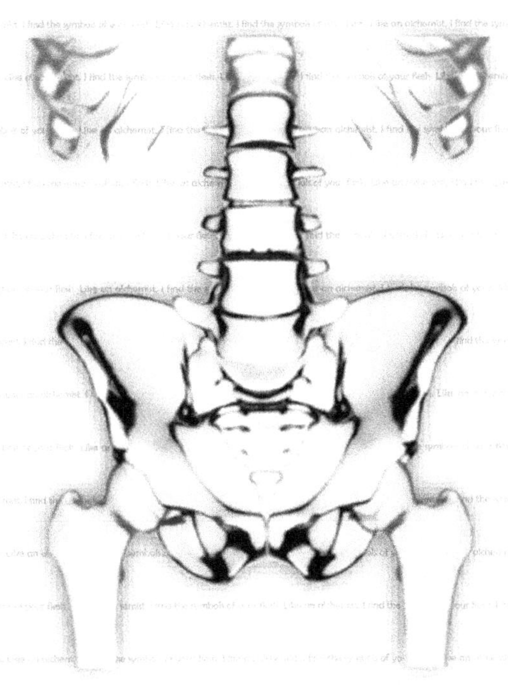

ABYSS

Ever wanted to stare into the abyss of another knowing full well
that the abyss stares back at you?
Ever wanted to hold another's spirit on the bow of your lips
knowing full well that one word would shake their world?
Ever wanted to be another's nothingness and everything...
a mass of cellular memory...
remembered in the touch of flesh?

CHAPTER II

THE
HIEROPHANT

CHANCE TAKER

You're driving me to insanity,
to the abyss, I know inside,
to that dark place,
where retreat is the only refuge.
Enjoy it you said,
live for each day.
Well, tell me then -
what of the eternity in your eyes,
the seeking in your skin -
the blind misguided consideration in your
movements.
What of your hopes?
What of your dreams,
or the seeds of dreams you have yet to imagine?
Speak to me then o' naked dancer - too controlled to be a chance
taker.
Speak to me of the lies you tell yourself at night when the moon
hangs like a soaked tea-bag in the flatness of the sky.

Going too far,
reaching the end.
Knowing the bloodletting about to begin but simply
relying on destiny.
Unbearable lightness,
indifferent wait?
Bring me your pain,
bring me your disappointment.
But, above all, bring me your confusion.

I have no fear of your inconsistency.
I am however terrified to be unbearably weightless,
in a world of insurmountable choices.

BIG WORDS

Life
Scattered pieces of jargon
floating on an amenable
sea of hope.
Love
Blissful ravishment,
tearing pieces,
stitching hearts.
Water bearer,
soul destroyer,
eater of lies,
harbinger of insanity.
Lust
Mystery unfolding over epochs,
blood water in the sand.
Eyes in the darkness,
breathing in the blackness.
Hands clasping hands in wet urgency.
Seduction
Dangerous game for intriguing minds,
spirits colliding in the night.
Souls in a f[r]iction of promise.
Hunter, hunted?
We all have a [p]reference.
When does it stop?
When is the stillness ignited into flame?
When does the flame find the perfect fuel?

That which quenches...
that which kills...

~ XXX ~

IRON LUNG

The texture of my heart finds its genesis in the texts of my mind.
A rapid wheel of words circling the circumference of my existential being.
Begging always for conception,
for equilibrium,
for birth,
...for a reader of cosmic divinity.
A sigh to echo through me like the cataclysmic hiss of an iron lung breathing
life into cadaverous flesh.

EYE OF THE BEHOLDER

I have shut my eyes to you.
Squeezed tight lids over hovering orbs that once adored you
in their looking.
Pulled flesh-shades low over rims once ringed with longing
for your kindness, your tenderness, your odium.
Firmly latched pale surrounds that once craved your touch.
No longer will you sleep between the shadows of my lashes,
cast on the cotton of a pillow shared by two minds.
I have shut my eyes to you my seraph,
but I fear
that in so closing,
I have abandoned part of myself to the darkness
in which
I left you...
...found you.

FEAR

Why do you fear yourself?
Your eyes avert every danger as if the blood in your veins burnt
with ash intent.
Do you feel loneliness,
the emptiness of unrequited passion?
Do you not feel the pain your eyes bring me?
Perhaps you fear rather the escape you see in mine.
Are you alone?
Are you loved?
Do you feel the ferocious arms of comfort around you, or do
you hold your own hand in the black of night, when the wolf
stares you in the eye and challenges you to feel?

Do you perhaps fear the depth within you?
The passion, the adoration, and anger, which lurk inside.
Do you perhaps fear how much I can make you scream at
night with the shades drawn around you, my hands left to
destroy your self-stigma?
You are passé my love.
Clichéd in the deepest sense of the word.

Your hands scare me, your eyes scorch me and yet I would
rather you burnt me than left me alone without the pleasure
of your mind.
I feel your heat on me.
What is wrong with wicked ways?
Faith alone cannot overcome everything.
Faith cannot dissolve your body... its slick, sticky lines... the smell of you on my
skin, the lust you burn with inside me.

It's cold here where I am, in the unhindered realms of my subconscious.

I wonder where you are.
Are you granting your favours to those unworthy, have your eyes swelled
once more with tears?

I cannot submit myself to myself once again.

So, sweet nemesis who never knew my love,
goodnight,
farewell.
May flights of angels wing you to your solace,
as flights of muses bludgeon me once more.

CHAPTER III

THE
LOVERS

DEVOTION

I worship at the altar of your name,
the red-stained slide of it passing my lips in a whisper.
Hushed by the sacred prayer of my longing.
In the moment between breaths, when you turn within the depths of my lungs
and travel the curvature of my tongue,

I am naked to you.

STOLEN ACHE

The half-cast shadow of your hand traces the inner sanctum of
my hip,
curved in surrender to the caress of your words,
holy water flowing over the ripples of my flesh.
I cup your face between the emptiness of my palms and taste the
dampness of your skin
- the osmotic sweetness of heat bound longing.
Between the plains of our wrapping
whispered promises form,
a pact solidified by the heat of the sheets sheltering our oblivion.
Within you, I see everything and nothing,
the stolen pain of your madness,
your sorrow;
naked and wanting.
I inhale, and the scent is devoid of form.
I exhale,
touch your lips to mine,
and in the space between our breaths,
I count the lines of your mind
with my tongue.

KNOTS

I know not if surrender to feeling is better than surrender to half.
To having but not feeling
...to feeling but not having.
You died to me eternities ago and yet your bones remain paleontological
treasures buried beneath my skin.
They reveal themselves in the erosion of your absence,
poke caverns into the strata of my life, thought, and breath.
Yet I silently surrender to the Shibari of your absence
...have mercy on me.

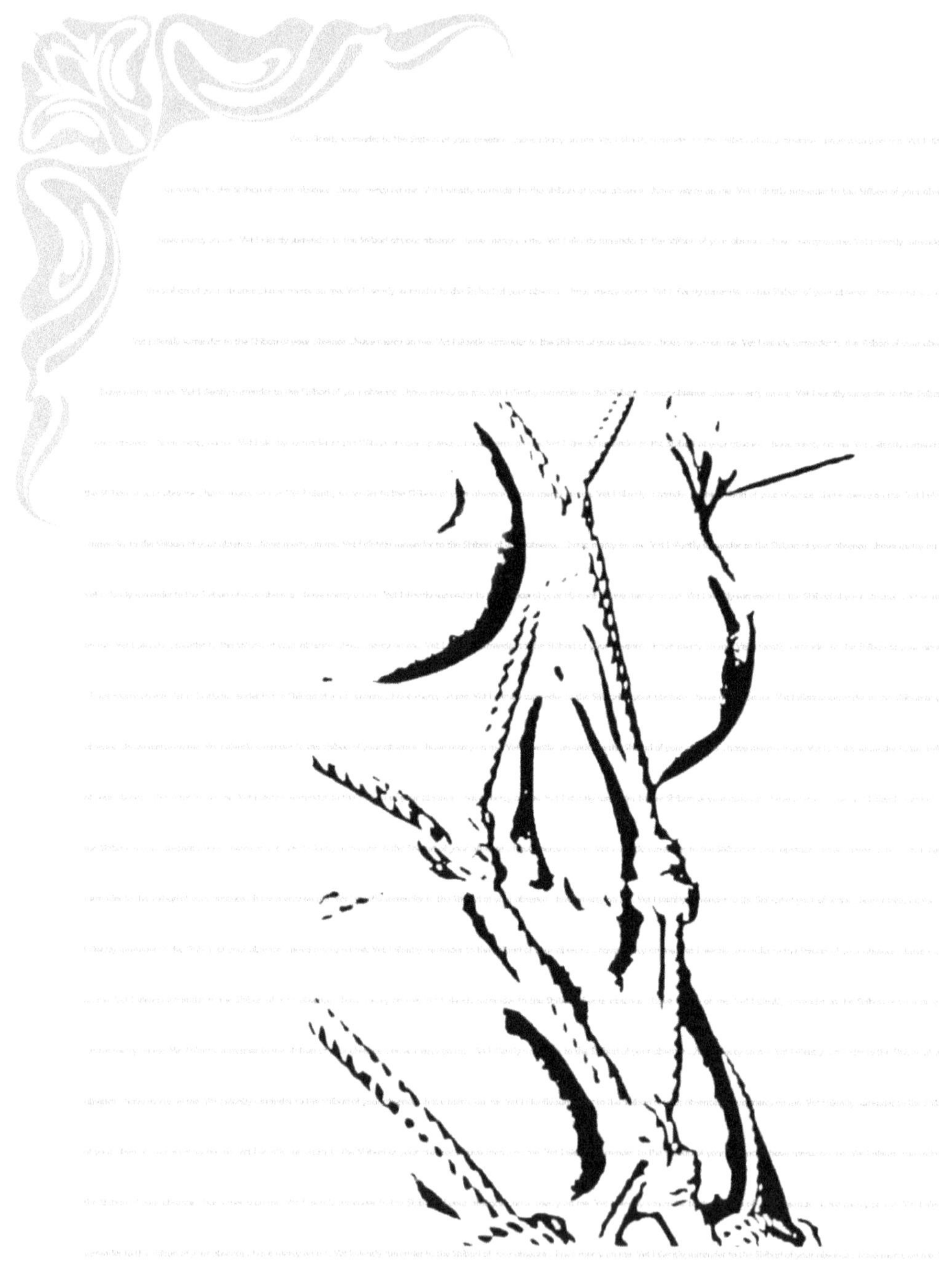

BLACK BIRDS

I hear two ravens moist against my mind.
One whispers purity the other wickedness.
Inside I wager and barter, trick and deceive.
All for one night of godless darkness
...a slick of black ink against my white canvas.
To see the butterflies of your eyes reflected on the cool steel of my silence.

NAPALM MANDALA

I look at you and see all the ways incisors can tear innocent flesh
I want to run my tapered hands under the primordial armour
plate of your ribs.
To blaze tempest kerosene down your atrophied spine.
I want to teach you that the greenish-blue hue beaten into your skin
is the infancy of your soul's mandala.
I want you to run Sanskrit ellipticals around my Jungian dreams and
find the wholeness of my psychic destruction.
To fill the corners and crevices of yourself with the vibrant Napalm
roaring on my night-black ocean.
I want to anarchize your nervous system, hollow your clavicles, and build a
bridge through the Nine Gates of Delhi,
to make a prison of your scapula where I lay my Isis lips.
I want your eyes to carry the black silt Nile,
your thighs strung beneath me like a ruby spear shot from a centaur's bow.
May the universe create a blueprint on the black pearled centre of your
labyrinthine heart.
May the violent cacophony of your spirit-sacrifice fracture my alchemical
elixir.
When you finally exhale and scatter your soul-sand to the gales, I want to
stand back and shiver
...at the shape of your horizon.

BORROWED STRENGTH

In the still blackness, there is a silence that very few know.
In the extremity of sound, a simplicity fewer understand.
Do you feel through my eyes?
Do you see through my skin?
Do you touch the sensuality of the earth; smell the ancient glimmering
of cataclysms of sand?
Two thoughts ahead, two steps behind!
Four pieces of rubber on an uneven foundation, as if the earth denied
entry.
Darkness surrounds and yet there is trust in fear.
There is coldness beneath me, draining the flame of my mind, complementing
the psychosis of my abyss.
Smooth roughness, the rage of emptiness, the beginning of perception?
Eerie, hallowed ground calls my name on the breeze; I devour the nearness of
oblivion.
The spirit takes flight within me like a marble heron breaking the trap of its
crumbling skin, escaping the bondage of its wings.
To be caught between the spirit and the dust is to know the purity of essence,
the triviality of time.
The ground shifts beneath me; subtle movement caught by the slivered moon.
The cosmos speaks forgotten tongues, a tremor of sound passing through
layers of whiteness before me.
The soul knows no frontier as it feels the dry sand around it.
The safe entrapment is seductively sweet as I seize the tempi of the earth's
dance within me,
The whirlwind inside howls as it touches the futility of my skin, the enclosure of
my body.
I see eyes in the darkness, the raising of wings, the craving flame.

I watch as the concrete takes flight and eyes beseech me to be still.
The flickering f[l]ame seduces me.
There is never benediction without malediction.

~ xlvi ~

To the right of my center time is twisting, wrapping its legs around the air in moist urgency; to the left silence, tranquility enveloped in the skin, beauty transcribed in surrendered ease.
The presence shapes around me, the soul is abated, the fury calmed.
I open my palms to caress the heavens; the energy of form, vague yet real.
The scent is rich and pervading as I look towards you and complete the circle in my mind.
The darkness chases as I sit still and fear living, yet still, I have métier to place my promise on the air, gift to know that in your simplicity is peace, in your stillness extremity and in your mind
surrender.

THE RHYTHM OF YOUR BODY

You begin slowly,
shifting fog on dew-soaked grass.
Your touch is light,
a feather grazing the air in descent.
My mind is lost completely in the shadow of your breathing.
Your lips touch mine and the world ceases.
Your hands dance on me,
snowflakes falling onto the water.
Your eyes graze mine,
lion purveying the grassland.
In the intensity of your eyes, I see
my mind unfold, yielding, opening
to you like the starch
whiteness of salt land.
I slide my hand down the tender slope of
your back and search the crevices of your flesh.
I am lost in you.
Your breathing becomes the slow trickle
of a mountain stream as my craving boils
over the rim of our cup of restraint.
I watch your body as you touch me, the rise
and fall of your labour, the flush of your skin,
and the shadow of your shoulders.
I sense the rhythm in you, stirring, rising,
torrential storm soaking all that bids it stop.
At the moment when your eyes float to thoughts
unknown, I know you are challenging Titans to
battle.
You close your eyes to the world and give
yourself to the movement.
In that instant of implosion,
that second of retreat,
I know one simple truth:

~ xlviii ~

you make me sick because I adore you so.

~ xlix ~

~ xlix ~

MY SOUL TO PURITY

I know you are paddling in a pool of doubt.
You admit to old fears and retreating footsteps.
You will destroy this happiness; you will widen this chasm,
already three inches have become ten.
I do not pretend to understand your motivation, but I know that
what is between us is anathema to you.
Despite the restlessness, I will wait,
wait for you to tear my soul to shreds, to consume my heart and wretch
my spirit.
A first love is a thing of beauty,
is a thing to cherish,
is a thing to feel pain for,
to wait for...
a thing to lose?

I DO

I understand that indifference is default but that both happiness and sadness
are matters of choice.
I admit that my real purpose is not to submit to your judgement but for a
moment to be still and consider if I would ever actively seek it.
I acknowledge that I am forever standing half submerged by dark and half
embraced by light – neither defines my being.
I know the inner limitations of my character and am wise enough to know
that these confines are mine alone and cannot be compensated with you or
by you.
I have encountered my obstacles but wish no more to carry yours than you do
mine.
I have experienced my darkness and much prefer the light although I am
content that inside all humankind is the potential for harm.
I am cognizant of my potential to love and in that, I comprehend that I can
differentiate the soul from the mundane nature of lust.
I am versed in the language of manipulation but prefer the subtlety of
acceptance over persuasion.
I think deeply, worship unconditionally, and believe that perfect happiness is
possible - fleeting but exquisite and worth the search.
Neither statuesque nor a bombshell but strident in acceptance of my flesh.
In summation... I am...
nothing more and nothing less.

DO YOU

Do you delve the recesses of your mind to meet the beauty of the
spoken word?
Do you love with abandon?
Do you leave your hurt at the moment it found you?
Do you seek to know the character with mind before mouth?
Do you know how to read the cantos of the eyes before you hear
the sound?
Do you acknowledge that values are expansionists and can
incorporate all beliefs?

~ li ~

YOUR UNUSUAL

I don't know your unusual from your spoken word...
from your postures...
from your movements...
from your presence...
But when my day looks variegated...
when my time feels divergent...
when all I want to do is kiss the space where you wear your angel...
it is then that I know your unusual...

~ liv ~

CHAPTER IV

THE
DEVIL

COMING

Coming and going.
Toing and froing.
You arrived and you left.
You came and you went.
Mores the pity it took me three body lashes to realise...
you were infinitely more beautiful going...
than you ever were coming.

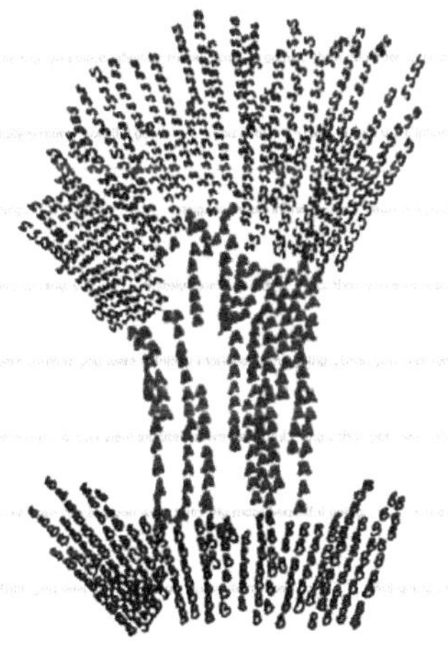

COGNAC

My mad thoughts conjured you into being,
...stitched you,
...scaffolded you into a Gordian knot of cognac candied lips,
gaping grotesque eyes,
and groping silly hands.
Legs all bandied and burgundy wined.
Yet oh, how quickly you learned to waste what you might have
savoured.

LIES

You celestial troglodyte
with your jaw full of withered stars.
Stars dead in their flickering -
forgotten in their ever expansion into the void.
Your lips may be coated in cosmic dust but the iron you taste is not star-
powder but rather the bitter ash of the burnt-out corpse of your lies.

~ lix ~

STREETCARS AND OIL STAINS

I dumped your broken body on a long-forgotten street.
Left you as an ornament for a wet sidewalk crowd.
Surrounded by a thousand footprints,
palm prints,
and a city swell of bodily fluids.
No detection of crime will trace my hands back to you.

At autopsy, a haggard face will intone in bored, unmarked voice
"...cause of death inconclusive, no cuts, lacerations or internal wounds".
Indeed, no microscope will find my fingerprints squeezed tightly around your
sunken heart.

I left you on a pavement where only time,
and sorrow,
and absence...
will ever mark your name.

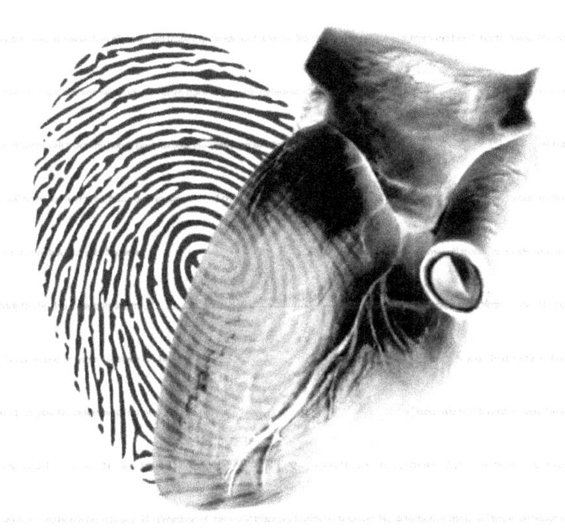

BURNING

Ambush me in the dark,
in tight corners
and ragged alleys.
Drape your robe over my regal shoulders,
as I wrap my corset ribs over your Pompeii legs,
and form a crown of lips for your head.

SPIRIT

Eyes...

There are no eyes here
in this valley of dying stars,
in this broken jaw of a lost kingdom.

Lips...

There are no lips here
in this doorway of creation,
in this star of unyielding passion.

Bodies...

There are none.
No perfection on this planet of confusing reality.
There are no jewels, no great king's golden coins, no boundaries, and no restriction.
No rulers of nations created by stupidity, there are no angers, no wars.
No innocent blood, no salty tears of those wounded, no graves for un-beating hearts.
But here there is love, for in the beginning, before man and his dark foreboding there was

Spirit...?

SMOKE

Envious eyes dart the ravines of my lips
craving the same embrace that I cavalierly bestow on the
cigarette resting there.
But I am not an anomalous curiosity to be solved, to be
entertained, to be exploited...
you fear me only because I am free.

CYANIDE

Illuminate the path of your forgotten feet.
If your light is worthy... perhaps
perhaps...
I will use my hands to teach you...
what turns me on...
under my cyanide stars.

TONIGHT

Tomorrow dear one, I may want to stroke your flesh for languid hours that
slip into clocks of liquid eternity.
But tonight... tonight,
I want to scratch the plaster from the wall behind my bed,
baptise your hair with the snow flecks of paint and shards of wood from
beneath my scarlet nails.
Tonight, I want to taste the acrid ash of your name with every naked breath.

NEWSFLASH

You stood before me,
destruction spread around you.
How empty is your mind?
How cold your spirit?
Your soul lacks substance, the image of purity that links me to my
skin.
Everything in you is stony,
icy like a wet mirage on boiling sand.
It drives you to insanity that "our" memories do not haunt me.

Newsflash: nothing of you ever came close to unnerving me, nothing stirs
within - nothing.
You depleted me,
took my very being and twisted it to suit your perversity,
bent me to your shape,
annihilated the very thing that makes me love.
You said I misled you,
you said I kept you for a fool!

Newsflash: the only thing I held for a fool was myself. The only thing I misled
was a fearful mind, tried to convince myself that I could find something in you
to love, find something to fulfill me, find something to give me a tenth of the
happiness of your absence.
I realised almost too late that I can never love the mundane, the thing that
holds you tightly like a hand of water squeezed into a fist.
You never understood,
you held too tight.
How much will it take for you to realise that you held me briefly, but you will
never possess me?
You wish me ill,
you wish me pain,
you wish me unhappiness.

Newsflash: that's all I've ever known living in your fucked-up reality. You may
know my thoughts, but my secrets are mine, secrets that fuel me, fear me,
that drives me.

You will never know the eternities within me,
the voices echoing in the darkness.

Most importantly you will never know me.

What you know is my falsity,
my pity,
the minuscule etchings I made within the lunacy of your selfishness.
You cannot see beneath my skin, round the walls guarding my eyes.
I fed you bits of truth and you molded them into your reason for being.

Newsflash: you never inspired the words within me, you never touched the
tender recesses of my naked spirit; all you saw was an image, a presentation,
a drumbeat on a wall of sound.
All you ever created was fear, doubt, illusions of love, deceptions of
complexity.
When I faced you today I finally understood the meaning of the Cheshire cat's
smile.
Smiles hide the truth — there is no eternity in love — only the pictures we feed
it.

Newsflash: some pictures have no effect because they lack power. You
cannot scratch my surface and that is why you see only lies in my
words.
Do you want the truth?
Then here it is.
I lied to you.
I spoke the words you wanted to hear and led you through a
brier of existence and tried to change your perceptions.
I manipulated your softness to see how much you were capable
of feeling and all the time stood still and blocked the connection
between my mind and heart.
I lost myself to your idiocy, to your willingness to give.
I pushed you to the brink then pulled you
back just to see how far you
would go.

~ lxix ~

You were (are) blind to me.
Despite your accusations, I can
feel,

more deeply than anyone on the periphery of your blackness.

Newsflash: I am abundantly grateful to you for teaching me one
simple lesson — it is no longer necessary to stand still and fear the
blackness.
I wish you the greatest happiness,
may you find the acceptance you ache for,
may you know the harshest pain and yet taste its languid surrender.
May you feel tenderness without reading the words that present it.
May I fade from your heart like a favourite melody.
May the print of my hand wash away in the saltiness of your tears.
May you find the peace of knowing.
May you lift your eyes and know the hills.

Goodbye.
Farewell.

SAMENESS

The red w[h]ine seeps – stained blood on your white lips.
Frozen in fruit ripe samplings of the
dead,
red,
curdled
emptiness of your soul
...a ghost of a shadow
...colour stained on skin.
The air is still and solid as you feed.
Thanatos entombed in purgation.
Sustenance confined in flesh.
Yet you sacrifice your soul for the sanity of...
SAMENESS.

LONGING

I miss you.
Not the shadow thing you are currently wearing.
You... my, you...
now (yesterday)... now (yesterday)... forever (tomorrow)... forever (tomorrow)...
you.
I once offered my love to you as a gift in small shaking hands...
In return, you offered your rage in a triumphant salute to your abhorrence.
Yet you remain my unfinished heartbeat.
Remember my love, young hearts forgive easily,
but old hearts grow deceitful with longing.

DEMIURGEOUS

I shower my lover with my hair until he is perfumed with its scent.
I am cleaved to his thighs and my mind is full only with the Kinbaku-bi of his
love,
the lightning storm of his lust
...an apostate pagan at the feet of the gods
I worship but one.

SAFFRON SMILE

I want a blue dress with reams of saffron lace widening the
skirts around my thighs.
I want to hear a rustle when I stalk towards your indomitable
frame.
I want to feel your heat through its lurid, tacky seams.
I want you to follow the line of its design over the slope of its
content.
I want to wear it until your scent embroiders its weave.
I want a blue dress.
I want to wear it until you tear it from my flesh and expose me to
your want.

VOODOO

In the closed grip of my iron palm, your flesh becomes malleable.
The rapping of my knuckles against the crimson wetness of your soul directs
mind ravens to flight,
imbues your inertia with a river of fire.
My Marie-Laveauesque power consumes from you
...forces your lavender scented pupils to contract and inhale,
all the while accepting that true knowing exists only when the black-night
birds respire, and return once more, to their cave of wanting.

MOLASSES

The warm molasses of my fingers
trace the contours of your languid skin.
I drum my ancient palms against your fullness with all the
delicious grace of a hand moved slowly,
delve your empty soul with my combative flesh and yet...
I am left with little more than bitter crystals from your cup of eternity
...spoken for,
...drunk dry,
...empty,
...taken.

HOLLOWS

When you
pull me towards you,
when you make your way into me,
when you make me...
Your sandstorm builds
grain upon unrelenting grain.
You gain in circular swirls of centrality,
a cavernous desire that besets all things that have goals.
You strip the truth from my bones,
the honesty from my skin.
You make me hollow with your nothingness
...inside of me.

CHAPTER V

THE
HIGH
PRIESTESS

SULTRY

This sultry night draws tides of darkness to the nude shore of your sacred oasis;
sketches a mirage on the primal vegetation of your soul eroded by the venom
of the past.
I lap in gentle waves against the nude iridescence of your flawless blueprint,
eroding your boundaries, shaping your scars, and meandering into your
Icelandic horizon.
All the while blazing pathways and igniting the pyro-techniques of your
synapses.
Tonight, I will whisper a hushed prayer to Kronos as I stare into the dark;
trusting the glimpse of you in Geminids shower.

WORSHIP

You worship but two things in life.
Woman and power.
In a hierarchy, you favor the latter over the former.
Your ambition outgrew mine and so you outgrew me.
Mores the pity you did not see that your preferences both reside
within me.

WILT

It seems you must have as much of life as four men.
And yet you are shocked when I want as much as four women.
Perhaps your fear is rather that I demand the power of four within your sole
wilted body.
Your celestial crazy and woodland wild.
Your teasing tentacle wide embrace.
Your half an hour in heaven before the devil knows you're dead.
will steadily unpick the stitches of your spine and unravel the threads of your
nervous system.
I will use those red sinews to unpick your name that is wedged between my
teeth.

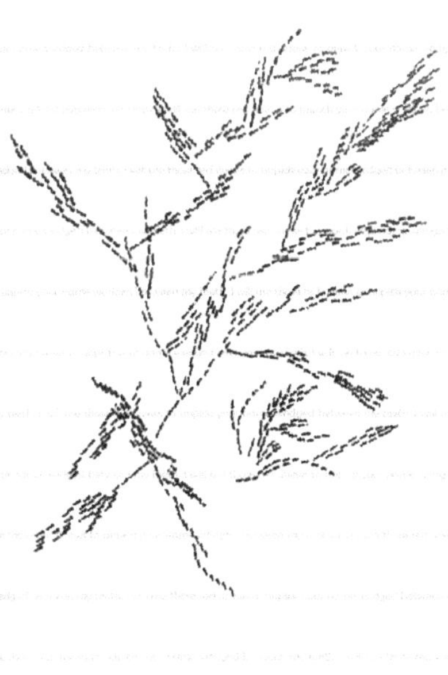

GOING TO WAR WITH THE STARS

You breathe a battle cry
formed on the Regulus question mark of your mouth full of stars.
In scarlet hues, you decry your Scorpius Titans.
Implore my gladius to shield the maleficent yearning behind the
vein-beat of your succulent thighs.
Now my Romulus you want my silence.
Now my Remus you want my solitude.
Yet how easily you forget.
I am undeniably a legionnaire's holy-land.
You, indisputably a leonine presence.
And once,
just once,
you called my stars to war.

PONDERING

I ponder the names you have been called through your eons of searching – those common to station in life – daughter, sister, lover – those darker names left unsaid? Yet in the lazy stretching of your claws, I see another picture. You tell a story with your succulent mouth and saccharine eyes and only a select group will ever realize that the script of your eyes and the sounds of your mouth are narrating two distinctly different stories. Between the defenses of the tale told by your tender lips, I see the emotional clarity of ideal belief, of conviction in love, of acceptance when shorn, of trust in man, of the fortification of a mother, the abiding love of a wife, the quietude of a sister and the restrained resonance of a daughter. Yet those eyes still speak an ancient language full of ripe tales and untamed hungry craving!

THE CRONE

The shadow of my past is written on your present.
One day when this body goes to ruin will you still trace your mouth along its dilapidated lines?
Will you run your hands along its seams stitched in failing flesh?
Will you seek the heart of the warrior within the crone... the venerated... the despised?

YOU DO NOT KNOW

You have asked me to fight against my nature, to rage against
my biology, my cellular memory, by forgetting you but
continuing to worship at your dais.
Do you not see the discontinuity of what you want from me?
Have you no concern for the destruction of your need for me to love
without vilifying you.
To share your softness without acknowledging the curve of your
mouth and the heat of your leg beside mine, in weak surrender.
I admire your need to control the way I feel...it must be intoxicating in
the case of a woman who can bend her will to yours and allow you to
hold control in the palm of your overly-lined hands.

You force my mind to coldness.
I dreamt last night of ice,
of slip-sliding without grip over the blackened tiles of your deceit.

Yet I want to rage at you in the normalcy of womanhood.
I want to accuse you of not knowing what love is...
of not knowing how to feel or what feelings are
and yet..., and yet...,
the time has come to admit that you do know,
you know all of this...
you simply do not love me.

~ XC ~

TWIN HEARTS

I have a heart that beats in two places.
It is neither torn nor confused.
It does not rip asunder the lustography of my soul rhythm.
It simply taps in two streams of being.
One reverberates in forests and lakes and burnt desert sand.
The other finds solace in the events of necessary duty.
Do you judge my endless incompleteness,
my sudden disregard for your thought-light emptiness?
Do you desire to see me nailed to your plinth of normalcy?
Do you want to tame the desolation within me which simply evokes
your lack?
Go ahead my love, but always remember that I have a heart that beats in
two places
and only one will atrophy under your g(r)aze.

CHAPTER VI

DEATH

END POINTS AND STARLIGHT

The distance between a star and its birth throws millennial shadows across the
craters of your regret.
You are ever diminishing in your movement away from your source.
Yet at séance, I seek you.
In cards, I call your fatalism to cross my destiny.
In leaves and grains, my eyes burn your lips onto sacred porcelain.
Would that I could draw your hush into me.
Wrap your spine with my sorrow stained thighs.
But you my deathly pale moon cannot be found in unearthly realms.
You have long since fled in return to the dark of your distance.

DESTRUCTION

So many thoughts clouding the mind, jumbles of jigsaws floating
in incandescence.

Selection of images.

There is a savage paradise in the Sapphic theater of red – BULLSHIT
– lines drawn in the sand.

I bought a happy home, encased in pink and brown, white picket
fences, sweet peas on the vine.
And yet my heart is breaking.
And yet my heart is breaking.

I cannot search if I do not know me.
People pleaser?
People pusher!
I perfect your life and fuck your soul.
I do it again and again and again.
A pound of flesh for a pound of flesh.
I take as I give.
My words.
My thoughts.
My abyss.
I took your soul and molded it to my vanity.

It is easier if they die – your perfect creations.
It is far easier to kill their spirit with each word – each perfect discontent.

I hate your wrongness.
Conjunctions fucked in hatred.
Red stained on white.
Blood on a toilet seat.

**Seeping truth.
Speaking lies.**

**I need a distraction.
Maybe unconditional love is undeliverable.**

~ xcix ~

TRIDENT

I am being held
here.
Being loved here.
Being scared here.
Being shot here.

I am lost here.
Found here.
Disturbed here.

Here.
Now.
There.
Never.

Take my hand.
Short space in time.
Enough?
Are you mine?
In every moment.
Every breath.
Every truth.
Every smile.
I cannot make you mine.

I can't leave.
I can't stay.
Go.
Go.
Mind/heart.
Hunter/hunted.
Giving up.
Letting go?
You will go on.

You will forget.
Rescue you.
You rescued me!

Don't go.
Don't hold on.

One stream.
One rhythm.
One flow.

Two lines.

Three foundations.

GHOSTS

In every beginning, there is an end.
In every end, there is an opportunity to find meaning in the
bluntness of
being,
thinking,
feeling.

Reality – your prime principle of ignorance.
Your false perception created by time.
Concrete.
Hard.
Endless.

Your ghosts evade your walls and perch upon your flesh.
Goodness, truth and being encased in a cage of dimness.
Blackness robed in sanity.
Sanity trapped in sweet surrendered...
ownership.

PANDORA

The curtain is falling
over the shapes of my mind,
blinding the truth of self,
within the strangeness of your emptiness.
You are the welcoming of an unsolicited spirit
wrapped in the cocoon of my blackness.

Whine, whine, whine... on and on and on...
Words fall like whispers on the filament of my mind
drawing sanity from me.

Where is my construct — my thought of self?
Actualization — flying, leaping, landing — back to the earth and her flatness —
stretched of nothing but yearning.
Yearning.
For more.
For less.
For me.
You drain my soul of sweetness, drop sorrow in your wake.
I cannot grasp the why of me.
I cannot blame you for all of Pandora's weakness and yet you are the
template within which I frame my thought.
Loneliness is an oil, which encases bones in darkness and yet within
your darkness lays the light of knowing the self.
Why lie through your sorrow?
Blame with your anger...
Scold with your words.

PALM TO PALM

You were there.
Darkness.
Void.
Hand to hand, as lover's hands do touch.
Reflection: your hand on mine.
Take it.
Make it.
Break it.
Tearing down, destroying.
Against nature.
Against life.
The rule of three.
Often defeated by the law of lust.
Can no longer analyse,
no longer, intellectualize,
the heat inside my mind.
Feeling.
Filtering.
Unable to reject.
Unable?
Unwilling?
Fine lines,
giant mistakes.
Blurring at the edges.
Turing in the mind.
Body and soul... separate?
Does not compute.
Does not integrate.
Give you my body without my mind
....mind without body?

SORROW RAIN

Loving you is like
driving a car on a dark
night in a
thunderstorm.

A part of
me is
petrified that I
cannot see before
me - I want the
inexorable
beating of the
rain to cease.

I know dawn
will soon break
and the clouds will
clear and with them,
the road will seem an
island.

And yet there is part of
me that tempts the moon
to hang in the sky and the
water to torrent down
over the earth without
end
because your
love is
conducting an
orchestra in the
orgasm of a lightning
storm, howling aloud
at the electric blue
of the sky even
when your voice
is soaked in
sorrow.

REPENT

I spread the vestiges of my regret at the coastline of your shore
and forever darken your waters with my shadow.
Yet your skin-servants still carry you towards me on a platform of
your pain.
In my ferocity,
I take your flesh
and cloak
my hollow bones.

~ cix ~

LIMELIGHT

You implode inside of me
- limelight on a dew-lit night.
Shards of your splintered soul travel the path of my veins in all the
vitriol of their sharpened edges.
You are fragmented,
...unfinished,
...mirror glass collapsed in violent anger.
Yet you seek a path into my sacredness.
Your destination my mind, not my heart.
Within my skull, I turn you like a child's kaleidoscope.
I see your brokenness, your scattered parts like stars rattling the doors of
heaven.
I see, I see, I see...
and yet I do not know.
Because in the darkness your emptiness becomes mammoth
...becomes...
becomes.

~ CX ~

MEDITATION ON PAIN

I may never grow old with you but the moment I inhale my last
breath
your face will appear before mine.
In that exquisite instant, I will know
that I knew what it was to be both
loved and hated at the same moment.
My death
holds no power
over your pain.

SURRENDER

Beauty will always bring cathartic destruction.
Therefore, I do not get close to humans.
They are not interesting enough to be beautiful,
ergo not beautiful enough to be destructive.

CHAPTER VII

THE
HERMIT

PRESENCE

I feel your presence in the grit of the sand running between my fingers.
The roughness is the turmoil of your mind trapped within silicone spheres of damp earth.
I smell you in the eagerness of the grass growing high on the dunes.
Your soul lingers in the undercurrent of evolution manifest in the ever-shifting expanse before me.
I see you written on the ocean like a stretch of skin.
Your body travels with the undulation of the waves beating back the strength of the inescapable.
I taste you on my lips like the briny mist of the ocean-deep raging before me/inside me.
The salt and the sand, the salt and the sand...
and the ever-growing presence...
Your absence is blatant in my presence like blood from an open wound, a cancerous invasion that will not heal.

WORDS

Some words are butterflies;
a few are great white sharks.
Roughly ¾ mere orgiastic nothingness.
One combined is all of these...
your name.
It taunts me with its purity.
No matter how many times I taste it I know but one thing...
I cannot undo you...
...I will never unknow you.

ON TIDES

Your tide-ripened lunacy cloys to the wet walls of the four
chambers of my enflamed psyche.
In the dank darkness of those claustrophobic dungeons of time, I
find the subtle freedom of madness.
It enrobes my flesh with a membranous welcome and bids me
...stay,
...search,
...seek,
...surrender.

Stay
Seek
Search
Surrender

FLUORESCENCE

Am I a native of your land?
Do I speak the tongues that dance on your shore?
Do I wash my skin in the tumultuous ebbing and gritty sands of
your safe harbour?
Do I stalk the steppes of your monotone tundra?
Do my feet breach the vastness of your glacial arms wrapped around
the dermis of your hills and valleys?
Do I slip through the tides of your oceans like a moray eel electrifying
you with the possibility of fluorescence?
Am I the native or the traveller
...the journey or the path
...the thought or the word?

GODS AND SAND

You are the desert of my mind.
You lie unobtrusively across the continents of my body and
silently await the coming of the hanging moon.
She touches you in darkness and,
all at once,
you ignite with the ferocity of Apollo,
swirling in the fantasy of your endlessness.
Like Aphrodite's skirt, you gather the storm to your breast,
one grain at a time,
until you are filled
with the pregnant silence of the universe.

SEPARATE SEEKING

I search for you on the streets of your native land.
I read the colours and seek the warmth of your blush on the face of strangers.
My hands reach out to grasp your enormous spirit within the dark eyes of others.
My mind screams for the stability of your unhinged mind.
In all of this, I know that I cannot breathe your power by osmosis.
I cannot taste you in the tributary of another.
I cannot roll your stones against the shore of a foreign land.
They are not you.

UNKNOWN

Your solitude
a whispering Neanderthal,
enraptures,
-   a quill to the ink of my being.
The mirror glass of your eternity reflects against me,
merciless shards of soul-silver rip the fabric of time,
dare my mind to [in]consequential action.
You stir within me, a river of perpetuity tapping the shores of infinity,
begging for an embrace.
You are the known
...the treaded earth of my history,
...a repetitive climb of my mountainous spirit.
Yet you are new
...isolated against the hamlet of my fury.
You know not my ineptitude.
Yet you label me as dull-witted,
...as insecure,
...a boat against the oceans rage.
Yet still, you seem to think I need you...;
perhaps you are correct,

...perhaps I need your blackness to justify my own.

INSANITY

You are my Rorschach.
You create shadows with the ink of your words.
How do I analyse the stain you leave on the paper of my heart?

www.ingramcontent.com/pod-product-compliance
Lightning Source LLC
Chambersburg PA
CBHW061737050726
47598CB00002B/518